GAO

United States General Accounting Office

Report to the Chairman, Committee on Government Reform and Oversight, House of Representatives

January 1995

HAZARDOUS WASTE INCINERATORS

EPA's and OSHA's Actions to Better Protect Health and Safety Not Complete

GAO/RCED-95-17

United States
General Accounting Office
Washington, D.C. 20548

Resources, Community, and
Economic Development Division

B-257938

January 25, 1995

The Honorable William F. Clinger, Jr.
Chairman, Committee on Government
    Reform and Oversight
House of Representatives

Dear Mr. Chairman:

In 1990, the Environmental Protection Agency (EPA) became concerned about workers' safety at hazardous waste incinerators because of the possibility that waste handling operations could pose a significant health threat to employees. As a result, EPA requested assistance from and established a joint task force with the Occupational Safety and Health Administration (OSHA) to evaluate compliance with relevant health and safety requirements at hazardous waste incinerators. The task force's 1991 report summarized the results of inspections at 29 such facilities and made five recommendations to EPA and four to OSHA.[1] These recommendations were intended as follow-through measures to correct violations detected during the inspections, educate the combustion industry, improve the coverage of inspections, educate compliance officials, and prompt EPA to conduct research and revise incinerators' permits as necessary.

In response to your request for information on whether hazardous waste incineration facilities are following federal health and safety requirements, we determined (1) what the status of the task force report's recommendations is, (2) what the results of subsequent inspections and enforcement actions at the 29 facilities have been, and (3) whether EPA or OSHA have taken other actions beyond those recommended by the task force to better protect health and safety at hazardous waste incineration facilities.

Results in Brief

EPA and/or OSHA have fully implemented three of the task force's recommendations: EPA and OSHA have followed up on violations found during the task force's inspections, EPA and OSHA have educated the combustion industry, and EPA has taken additional steps to educate compliance officials. EPA has not fully implemented other

---

[1]Of the 29 facilities originally inspected, 8 facilities ceased operating their incinerators. Of the remaining 21 facilities, none was specially constructed for the specific purpose of remediating Superfund wastes—wastes from sites being cleaned up under the Superfund program and administered by EPA. Rather, 9 are private facilities that only incinerate waste generated on-site, none of which is Superfund waste, and 12 are commercial facilities that accept waste generated off-site, some of which may be Superfund waste.

recommendations to (1) improve the coverage of EPA's inspections and (2) conduct research on the use of certain operating equipment and revise incineration facilities' permits, as necessary, to limit the use of this equipment. OSHA has not fully implemented the recommendations that it (1) educate compliance officials and (2) improve the coverage of its inspections.

Subsequent to the task force's inspections, EPA and the states inspected the facilities but did not detect the same pattern of violations. OSHA did not schedule further inspections for these facilities because the agency judges the relative health and safety risk of working at incineration facilities to be lower than the risk of working in other types of industries. Therefore, OSHA has assigned incinerators a low priority for inspections.

EPA and OSHA have taken several actions beyond those recommended by the task force to protect health and safety at incineration facilities. However, one of these actions—OSHA's plan to require facilities to have accredited training programs for workers who handle hazardous waste—may not achieve its intended result because OSHA does not have a viable plan to ensure that all hazardous waste facilities submit their programs for accreditation.

Background

The Resource Conservation and Recovery Act of 1976 (RCRA) authorizes EPA to set minimum operating requirements for hazardous waste facilities to protect the public and the environment. The Occupational Safety and Health Act of 1970 authorizes the Department of Labor, through OSHA, to establish standards to protect workers' health and safety. Under both statutes, states can be authorized to inspect facilities, take enforcement action against facility owners/operators, and assess penalties at facilities that fail to meet states' federally approved RCRA or OSHA programs. EPA has authorized 46 states to implement their own RCRA programs, and OSHA has authorized 23 states to implement their own OSHA programs. The federal government is responsible for implementing RCRA and OSHA programs in the remaining states.

According to EPA's general operating requirements for hazardous waste facilities, workers must be trained to know the environmental requirements that apply at their facility, and facilities must have contingency plans and emergency procedures for accidents. To ensure facilities' compliance with regulatory or permit-related requirements, EPA recommends that its regions or the states inspect facilities annually. Every other year, EPA recommends an in-depth inspection lasting several days, rather than the annual 1-day walk-through. Facilities that accept Superfund waste must be inspected within the 6-month period prior to receiving such waste. During inspections, EPA and the states complete checklists of items to review while observing facilities' operations and reviewing facilities' records and files.

OSHA's health and safety regulations are intended to ensure that employees can recognize and avoid unsafe conditions and are instructed in the handling of any special equipment, among other things. At hazardous waste facilities, employees must receive special hazardous material training. To ensure compliance with OSHA's regulatory requirements, federal or state OSHA inspectors conduct either "programmed" (planned) inspections or "unprogrammed" inspections to follow up on complaints, referrals, or accidents.

The scheduling of federal programmed inspections is based on industries' history of health or safety violations. Facilities within the types of industries that have a history of many violations receive programmed inspections for health or safety by OSHA's field offices. OSHA also reserves some resources to conduct programmed health inspections at randomly selected facilities having a history of few health violations. States may use different methods for scheduling programmed inspections. OSHA and the states conduct unprogrammed inspections in response to complaints, referrals, and accidents resulting in catastrophes or fatalities.

According to an OSHA Office of Policy official, during fiscal year 1993, about half of the inspections were programmed, or targeted, as a result of particular industries' violations. The remainder of the inspections were unprogrammed. OSHA's inspections rely on inspectors' observations as well as interviews with employees and reviews of records.

As of November 1994, 162 incinerators were operating in the United States. Of these, 141 had their final permits, which impose facility-specific operating requirements. The remaining 21 were considered in interim status. When an existing hazardous waste facility first becomes subject to RCRA's requirements for permits, it generally assumes "interim status" until its operator completes the permit application process. A facility under interim status is allowed to continue operating under general operating requirements, pending EPA's or the state's approval of the facility's final permits.

In May 1990, after local citizens and workers made complaints or allegations about waste handling practices at an incinerator in North Carolina, EPA requested that the Department of Health and Human Services' Agency for Toxic Substances and Disease Registry (ATSDR) evaluate health threats posed by the incinerator. Although routine RCRA inspections conducted while the facility operated from 1976 through 1989 had not detected or confirmed these allegations, ATSDR concluded that waste handling operations at the facility had posed a significant health threat to employees.

In September 1990, at EPA's request, OSHA and EPA formed a task force to evaluate compliance with health and safety requirements at 29 hazardous waste incinerators, including all commercial facilities with final permits, all facilities under interim status, and all incinerators burning Superfund waste. The task force's May 1991 report summarized the results of these joint inspections. In total, EPA and OSHA detected 395 violations. The task force's report made five recommendations to EPA and four recommendations to OSHA to improve the coverage of inspections and educate compliance officials and industry, among other things.

EPA and OSHA Have Fully Implemented Some Report Recommendations but Not Others

Of the task force's recommendations, EPA and/or OSHA have fully implemented three. However, the agencies have not fully implemented four other recommendations.

Recommendations That Have Been Fully Implemented

EPA's and OSHA's follow-up on violations. On the basis of the 75 RCRA violations detected, EPA and the states initiated enforcement actions and collected over $2 million in penalties. The violations detected include the facilities' failure to provide adequate environmental training and inability to respond fully to emergencies. OSHA and the states also completed enforcement actions for the 320 OSHA violations and collected $44,000 in penalties. The violations detected include the facilities' failure to provide adequate hazardous material training, conduct medical surveillance, or update contingency plans for emergencies.

EPA's and OSHA's education of industry. EPA and OSHA conducted outreach to the combustion industry to ensure the industry's compliance with their regulations. EPA and OSHA officials said they jointly wrote to combustion industry representatives to emphasize the importance of compliance with health and safety requirements. EPA also met with combustion industry representatives to tell them that the task force had found significant health and safety violations that needed to be addressed.

EPA's education of compliance officials. Following the recommendation that EPA improve its regional and state officials' knowledge about incineration, EPA developed a training program for and designated combustion experts for conducting inspections in each of the agency's 10 regional offices. These combustion experts meet regularly to discuss issues concerning hazardous waste incinerators and other combustion facilities.

Recommendations That Have Not Been Fully Implemented

EPA's inspection coverage. Although the task force's report recommended that EPA adopt some of the task force's inspection procedures so that EPA could better scrutinize industry's compliance with the agency's regulations, EPA did not fully implement the recommendation. In particular, the task force's inspectors used a new checklist that expanded the checklist used during EPA's routine inspections. This new checklist was designed to evaluate the effectiveness and not just the presence of employee training programs, contingency responses, and emergency plans. Furthermore, interviews of employees during the task force's inspections assessed employees' knowledge of environmental requirements and employees' ability to carry out contingency plans and emergency procedures. But in general, during routine inspections, EPA or the states only review employers' records to ensure that employers have a training program and that plans are on file.

After the task force made its recommendations in December 1990, an EPA Assistant Administrator sent a memo to regional administrators asking that they distribute the task force's inspection checklist and employee interview guide to their staff and the states. EPA's Technical Assistance Branch Chief also orally instructed regional enforcement section chiefs to include items from the task force's checklist in the regions' routine inspections. In addition, EPA included the new checklist in the agency's inspection training manual and training courses.

However, some of the EPA regions and states did not adopt the task force's checklist as suggested or directed because, according to regional compliance and enforcement officials, they were not aware of headquarters' instructions. Furthermore, according to an EPA Technical

Assistance Branch official, EPA headquarters did not follow up to ensure that inspection procedures were changed because EPA believed the changes would be made, since it included the checklist in the training manual and training courses. An EPA Technical Assistance Branch Chief said that even if regions and states had adopted the task force's checklist and interview guide, it would be difficult for inspectors to duplicate the information obtained during the task force's inspections because the inspections included both EPA's and OSHA's interviews and were very focused. However, according to a regional inspector, while time is a factor during inspections, interviews of employees could routinely be included in all inspections, routine or in-depth, or on a case-by-case basis. These interviews would help confirm industry's compliance with EPA's requirements and assess employees' knowledge of required duties.

As a result of our work, EPA's Assistant Administrator for Enforcement and Compliance Assurance issued a memorandum, dated September 23, 1994, to Regional Administrators and other RCRA officials requiring them to adopt the task force's inspection protocol, which includes using the revised checklist and employee guide, for workers' safety and health in regional RCRA Compliance Evaluation inspections. In addition, the memorandum requires that regional inspectors refer these violations to regional OSHA officials.

EPA's research on the use of certain operating equipment and review of permits. EPA did not fully implement the recommendation that it conduct research on the cause for and impact of using certain operating equipment—automatic waste feed cutoffs and emergency safety vents, or vent stacks—and that it reopen permits, as necessary, to address the use of this equipment. During the task force's inspections, EPA observed the frequent use of automatic waste feed cutoffs at about half of the 29 facilities and the frequent use of vent stacks at 9 of these facilities. Automatic waste feed cutoffs prevent waste from entering the combustion chamber of an incinerator when operating conditions fluctuate outside certain parameters, such as those for temperature. Vent stacks protect workers and equipment by releasing gases when equipment malfunctions. While both are considered safety devices, EPA considers their frequent use an indication of poor operating practices. In particular, the frequent use of waste feed cutoffs (1) may be a sign of unsteady operation and (2) may cause the residue to be treated less efficiently. Furthermore, gases released through vent stacks contain more hazardous particles than gases routed through the air pollution control devices.

In response to the recommendation, EPA conducted experiments at two of its research incinerators. However, because of funding and equipment limitations, EPA's initial tests did not fully answer questions about the effects of using waste feed cutoffs and vent stacks. EPA believed that states had taken steps to place controls on the use of these devices at the facilities that the task force had found to have the greatest number of cutoffs and releases. Because these tests were inconclusive and because EPA believed that states had taken steps to control frequent usage, EPA did not review or revise other permits to place controls on the use of this equipment at the other facilities that the task force had found to have an excessive number of cutoffs and releases. For example, at one facility that the task force found to have an excessive number of waste feed cutoffs, no action has been taken. State officials told us they wanted to place controls on the use of waste feed cutoffs and vent stacks at this facility, but because EPA's regulations do not specifically address controls over this equipment, the use of any such controls would have to be negotiated when the permit was renewed. In commenting on our report, EPA stated that its concern is not with the use of automatic waste feed cutoffs per se, but with facilities that may frequently use automatic waste feed cutoffs. This is especially true when facilities exceed their permits' operating limits if the waste feed cutoffs occur while waste remains in the system.

EPA drafted a policy memorandum in 1992 to provide guidance to permit writers so they could place proper controls on the use of waste feed cutoffs and vent stacks in new permits and permits for facilities requesting modifications. EPA did not complete the draft memorandum because of other priorities, such as the agency's need to work with the regions and states on implementing the newly issued boiler and industrial furnace regulations and focusing on site-specific incinerator issues. According to an official in the Permits and State Programs Division, EPA did, however, revise its permit writers' training to include guidance on controlling the use of waste feed cutoffs and vent stacks. However, according to a combustion expert and Alternative Technology Section Chief, a policy memorandum would further support regions' and states' efforts to place controls over the use of waste feed cutoffs and vent stacks. State officials expressed a desire for such guidance.

By December 1996, EPA plans to revise its 1981 regulations for incinerators to, among other things, clarify that exceeding a permit's operating parameters or bypassing the air pollution control device violates the permit regardless of whether an automatic waste feed cutoff occurs. In the interim, 21 incinerators currently are awaiting their final RCRA permits. In

May 1993, EPA placed a high priority on issuing permits for existing combustion facilities that do not have final permits. While EPA does not anticipate that all of these facilities will be granted permits by December 1996, it hopes to make substantial progress.

OSHA's education of compliance officials (inspection expertise). OSHA has not implemented the task force's recommendation that the agency improve its inspection expertise. According to an OSHA Office of Policy Official, a memorandum of understanding entered into with EPA's Office of Enforcement in 1990 might have resulted in improved inspection expertise and knowledge of hazardous waste incinerators' operations for OSHA. This memorandum provides a framework for exchanging information and technical and professional assistance, conducting joint EPA-OSHA inspections, referring violations to each agency, and coordinating compliance and enforcement information.

According to an OSHA Office of Policy official, although the memorandum was implemented, it did not result in improved inspection expertise or increased knowledge. A Senior Enforcement Counsel with EPA told us that EPA's Office of Enforcement did not have oversight responsibilities for inspection and enforcement activities at hazardous waste facilities. Furthermore, EPA's Office of Enforcement did not provide information to EPA headquarters' compliance staff who are responsible for directing EPA's regional compliance activities at hazardous waste facilities, including inspection and enforcement—which are conducted primarily at EPA's regional and state levels. Because EPA headquarters did not direct the regions to coordinate their inspections of combustion facilities with OSHA and the regions did not suggest that states coordinate their inspections of combustion facilities with OSHA, the memorandum was not fully carried out.

However, in June 1994, EPA consolidated inspection and enforcement responsibilities in the agency's new Office of Enforcement and Compliance Assurance. According to an EPA Senior Enforcement Counsel official and an OSHA Office of Policy official, the consolidation of the responsibility to develop policy and guidance for inspections and enforcement actions within the new office will aid in carrying out the purpose of the memorandum and therefore in meeting the intent of the task force's recommendation. Furthermore, in September 1994, EPA's new Office of Enforcement and Compliance Assurance directed regions to inform OSHA of any facilities found in violation of RCRA's health and safety requirements, as required by the memorandum of understanding.

In commenting on our report, OSHA stated that it has trained 245 federal and state compliance officers at its Training Institute to increase their knowledge of hazardous waste sites' operations. We recognize that OSHA does have a training program that disseminates knowledge of hazardous waste site operations for its enforcement officials and that this training program has continually been improved. However, our discussions with officials in OSHA's Training Institute and OSHA's Directorate of Policy and Office of Field Programs reveal that OSHA has not made any changes to the training given to its enforcement officials as a result of the task force's recommendations.

OSHA's inspection coverage. OSHA also has not implemented the recommendation that the agency improve the coverage of its inspections by specifically including hazardous waste incinerators on its lists of programmed inspections. The refuse systems industry, which includes commercial hazardous waste incinerators, had a priority ranking, in terms of relative risk when compared with other industries, of 122 out of 324 in fiscal year 1991, and 150 out of 372 in fiscal year 1992. Following the task force's report, OSHA instructed that in fiscal years 1991 and 1992, any programmed inspections conducted at facilities included in the refuse systems industry be limited to two sectors of the industry—"Disposal and Collection of Acid Waste" facilities and "Incinerator Operations" facilities. However, even though incinerators were given a higher priority for being inspected within the refuse systems industry, the refuse systems industry was not ranked sufficiently high enough, with respect to relative risk, to result in any programmed inspections at hazardous waste incinerators. According to OSHA's Director of Data Analysis, OSHA did not inspect incinerators under this initiative because few of OSHA's federal or state offices have sufficient resources to conduct health inspections at industries that are not ranked in the top 100. Following fiscal year 1992, OSHA no longer restricted inspections of refuse systems industries to facilities that dispose of or collect acid waste or that incinerate. Furthermore, in fiscal year 1993, the refuse industry's relative risk fell to 220.

Results of Subsequent Inspections and Enforcement Actions by EPA and OSHA at Facilities Inspected by the Task Force

Since the task force made its inspections, EPA and/or OSHA, and states have inspected 22 facilities that have operating incinerators.[2] However, the types of inspections conducted after the task force's inspections differed in scope from the task force's inspections, and EPA, OSHA, and the states have not detected as many or the same pattern of health or safety violations as did the task force.

Since 1990, EPA and the states conducted 108 inspections at the 22 facilities and detected 630 violations. These inspections found a wider range and variety of violations than the task force found. However, fewer violations have been detected in the categories that the task force assessed, including personnel training, contingency plans, and emergency response. While EPA said that this may be due, in part, to improvements in industry's training of its workers as a result of the task force's inspections, as noted earlier, EPA's inspections only determined whether training programs existed. On the other hand, the task force's inspections focused on the effectiveness of training for the workers. Furthermore, EPA's and the states' subsequent inspections were broader in scope and looked at all aspects of the facilities' operations. As a result, violations of a wider array of regulatory requirements were detected, including those for the facilities' noncompliance with permits, the management of containers, and incinerator operation requirements. These subsequent inspections and enforcement actions resulted in an additional $4 million in collected penalties. According to EPA and state officials, all but one of the incineration facilities have returned to compliance following these inspections. (App. I contains additional information on the number and types of violations detected during the task force's and subsequent inspections.)

OSHA and the states have conducted few health or safety inspections since the task force's inspections, and those that have been conducted were narrow in scope. OSHA and the states have not conducted any programmed health or safety inspections at the 22 operating incineration facilities since 1990 because the industries were ranked as a low priority, and they were not randomly selected for inspection. For example, in fiscal year 1993, OSHA's relative risk and priority ranking for commercial incinerators was 220 out of the 381 industries ranked. According to OSHA's Director of Data Analysis, it is not surprising that OSHA has not scheduled any programmed inspections at hazardous waste incinerators because of their relatively low risk and because of the low probability of their being randomly selected.

---

[2]Of the 29 facilities originally inspected, 22 received subsequent inspections. The remaining seven incinerators ceased operations prior to being reinspected. One of the 22 facilities that was subsequently inspected closed in 1991. Currently, 21 of the 29 facilities have active incinerators.

An OSHA Office of Policy official said that OSHA prefers to target its resources at industries that OSHA views as more dangerous to workers' health and safety, such as manufacturing and construction industries.

OSHA has, however, responded to eight complaints or referrals at five incineration facilities and collected about $22,000 in penalties. According to our analysis of the violations that OSHA found after the task force's inspections, none were violations detected by the task force at those five facilities. The violations have since been resolved. (App. II includes a comparison of health and safety violations detected during the task force's and subsequent inspections.)

EPA and OSHA Have Taken Other Actions Beyond Those Recommended by the Task Force

In addition to those actions recommended by the task force's report, EPA and OSHA have initiated other actions to protect health and safety at incineration facilities. EPA proposed a draft strategy for issuing permits to remaining incineration, boiler, and industrial furnace facilities under interim status and improving combustion regulations and policies. OSHA is planning to issue a regulation requiring hazardous waste facilities, including incinerators, to have accredited training programs for workers. However, OSHA has no means to ensure that all facilities submit programs and receive accreditation.

Partially in response to public concerns about incinerators and other types of combustion facilities, in May 1993, EPA issued a draft strategy for ensuring the safe and reliable combustion of hazardous waste. As part of that strategy, EPA designated the issuance of new incinerators' permits a low priority for 18 months so it could focus its resources on issuing permits for existing facilities under interim status, including the 21 discussed previously. In addition, the strategy calls for incorporating dioxin emission standards in new permits and incorporating more stringent controls over metals.[3] EPA has directed regions to use the stricter operating standards as guidance for writing and issuing new permits if permit writers determine that these new standards are necessary to protect human health and the environment. EPA also targeted combustion facilities, including a total of 10 incinerators and other hazardous waste combustion facilities, for two separate enforcement initiatives in September 1993 and February 1994. These initiatives focused primarily on hazardous waste combustion operations and resulted in EPA-and state-assessed fines of over $9 million.

---

[3]Dioxins are highly toxic organic compounds.

As directed by the Superfund Amendments and Reauthorization Act of 1986, OSHA is developing new standards and procedures for accrediting training programs for workers at hazardous waste facilities, including incinerators. OSHA expects this requirement to become final in December 1994. OSHA intends that the proposed regulation will result in workers' reduced exposure to hazardous substances and thus will help prevent fatalities and illnesses. Under the proposed regulation, all employees working on-site and exposed to hazardous substances and health or safety hazards will receive OSHA's accredited training. However, OSHA has no method to ensure that (1) all hazardous waste facilities submit training programs for accreditation and (2) all facilities' programs are accredited. OSHA and the states plan to rely on inspections to verify that facilities are complying with the requirement.

However, since 1990, OSHA and the states have conducted few inspections at hazardous waste incineration facilities, and given the relatively low risk that the agency assigns to incinerators, OSHA and the states would only conduct inspections at incinerators if they were randomly selected or in response to complaints, referrals, or accidents. EPA could be of assistance to OSHA to ensure that facilities have accredited programs by, for example, (1) verifying, during inspections by EPA and the states, whether training programs have received accreditation from OSHA and, if not, informing OSHA and (2) providing OSHA with EPA's hazardous waste facility identification data, which would give OSHA an inventory of such facilities that OSHA currently does not have. OSHA could use such information to track which facilities have not submitted training programs for accreditation. However, OSHA has not explored with EPA the ways in which EPA could assist OSHA.

Conclusions

EPA and OSHA have generally followed up on the task force's recommendations. However, EPA has not fully implemented two key recommendations that, in our view, could be undertaken relatively easily. In particular, some EPA regions and states have not adopted the revised checklist and employee interview guide as requested by EPA headquarters in December 1990, in part, because EPA did not follow up to ensure that regions and states did so. In response to our work, EPA recently issued another memorandum that specifically directs regions and states to adopt the task force's inspection protocol, which includes the revised checklist and employee interview guide. If regions and states follow through and implement this requirement, inspectors will be better able to determine not only that employees have received the required training but also the effectiveness of that training. However, because EPA issued this memorandum only recently, it is too soon to know if the regions and states will follow the agency's directive.

Furthermore, although some states took action to improve the operations of facilities that made frequent use of automatic waste feed cutoffs and vent stacks, EPA and the states did not revise permits at other facilities that the task force also found were frequently using this equipment. However, in 1992, EPA drafted guidance for permit writers to clarify the use of these operating devices in new permits and permits for which modifications were being requested, but it never completed the guidance. While EPA plans to revise regulations for incinerators that will clarify when this operating equipment can be used, at the earliest these regulations will not be completed until the end of 1996. In the meantime, EPA hopes to make substantial progress in issuing RCRA permits for 21 facilities under interim status. Without guidance to include controls on the use of automatic waste feed cutoffs and vent stacks, some of these permits may not include these stricter operating requirements.

OSHA plans to make one substantive improvement, as required by the 1986 Superfund amendments act, to improve workers' health and safety by accrediting hazardous waste training programs. Under current plans, however, the agency will have no way of knowing whether this requirement is actually being met. On the other hand, by working with EPA, either through the memorandum of understanding or directly with EPA staff, OSHA could explore what assistance EPA could provide OSHA to determine compliance with its accreditation requirement. This assistance could include relying on EPA and states to identify, through RCRA inspections, facilities failing to have OSHA-accredited training programs and refer them to OSHA.

Recommendations

To ensure that EPA regions and states comply with EPA's directive to adopt the task force's inspection protocol to assess the effectiveness of training for workers, contingency plans, and emergency preparedness, we recommend that the Administrator, EPA, follow up, after an appropriate interval, to ensure that federal and state inspectors include revised procedures in their inspections.

To ensure that permit writers have the necessary guidance to place controls on automatic waste feed cutoffs and emergency vent stacks prior to EPA's issuance of revised regulations for incinerators in 1996, we recommend that the Administrator, EPA, complete and issue the agency's draft guidance relating to waste feed cutoffs and vent stacks.

To ensure that all hazardous waste facilities' training programs receive accreditation, we recommend that the Secretary of Labor direct the Administrator, OSHA, to work with EPA to develop a means to ensure that all hazardous waste facility employers submit their training programs to OSHA and receive required accreditation.

Agency Comments

EPA and OSHA provided us with written comments on a draft of this report. EPA noted that some EPA regions and some states did not adopt or include the task force's inspection protocol, which includes the revised checklist and employee interview guide, in their routine inspections. EPA also concurred with our finding that EPA needs to provide guidance to permit writers on the use of automatic waste feed cutoffs and vent stacks. The agency plans to complete guidance and has included it in EPA's fiscal year 1995 plans. EPA's comments and our responses are included in appendix III.

OSHA generally disagreed that it did not fully respond to the task force's recommendations that it improve its coverage of inspections by including hazardous waste incinerators on its list of targeted inspections and that it improve the inspection expertise of its compliance officers. While we recognize that OSHA took some actions to carry out these recommendations, such actions neither resulted in any programmed inspections of hazardous waste incinerators, thus improving OSHA's coverage of inspections, nor improved inspection expertise. As discussed earlier, the memorandum of understanding between OSHA and EPA was ineffective in improving the inspection expertise of OSHA's inspection officers because no joint inspections were conducted at incinerators as a result of the memorandum. Also, while OSHA has made changes to its education curriculum, none resulted from the task force's report.

Furthermore, OSHA stated that its current plans to improve workers' health and safety by accrediting hazardous waste training programs will be sufficient along with industry outreach to ensure that the quality of employers' safety and health training programs will be enhanced. However, on the basis of our review of OSHA's methods of selecting facilities for inspections and OSHA's history of performing few inspections, we continue to believe that OSHA's current procedures will not ensure the fulfillment of OSHA's stated intent that all employees working on-site and exposed to hazardous substances will receive OSHA's accredited training. OSHA's working with EPA could provide an opportunity for that assurance. OSHA's entire comments and our responses to them are provided in appendix IV.

We conducted our review from October 1993 through December 1994 in accordance with generally accepted government auditing standards. Our scope and methodology for conducting this work are discussed in appendix V.

As arranged with your office, unless you publicly announce its contents earlier, we plan no further distribution of this report until 30 days after the date of this letter. At that time, we will make copies available to others on request.

Please contact me on (202) 512-6111 if you or your staff have any questions. Major contributors to this report are listed in appendix VI.

Sincerely yours,

Peter F. Guerrero
Director, Environmental Protection
 Issues

Contents

Appendix VI
Major Contributors to
This Report

Abbreviations

ATSDR	Agency for Toxic Substances and Disease Registry
EPA	Environmental Protection Agency
GAO	General Accounting Office
OSHA	Occupational Safety and Health Administration
RCRA	Resource Conservation and Recovery Act

Comparison of RCRA Violations Detected by EPA and States, 1990-93

Category of violations	Violations detected by task force's inspections 1990	Violations detected after task force's inspections			Total violations detected after task force's inspections
		1991	1992	1993	1991-93
Personnel training	14	1	2	3	6
Contingency plans/emergency response	16	5	4	3	12
General inspection requirements	12	40	33	32	105
Preparedness and prevention	17	17	9	10	36
Operational procedures	11	0	3	5	8
Incinerator requirements	5	7	5	19	31
Container management/ storage	0	54	13	53	120
Waste analysis plans	0	4	10	9	23
Incinerator permit	0	27	163[a]	8	198
Land ban	0	3	1	1	5
Falsifying records	0	6	0	0	6[b]
Other[c]	0	16	46	18	80
Total violations	**75**	**180**	**289**	**161**	**630**
Total inspections	29	35	34	39	108

Legend

EPA = Environmental Protection Agency
RCRA = Resource Conservation and Recovery Act

Note: In 1990, the joint task force detected RCRA violations at 21 of the 29 incineration facilities. Since that time, 8 of the 29 incineration units have ceased operations. Violations detected by EPA and the states after 1990 include those from inspections at the 21 facilities that still have active incineration units and 1 facility that ceased operations in 1991. According to EPA or state officials, all but one of the incineration facilities have returned to compliance following these inspections. This particular facility has historically had an excessive number of waste feed cutoffs and vent stack releases. The state has issued to the facility a stricter permit limiting the use of this equipment, and facility operations have improved.

[a]Over 150 of these 163 violations related to the use of vent stacks at one facility because the state-issued RCRA incinerator permit imposed limits on their use.

[b]These six violations occurred at one facility. The state and the facility agreed to shut down the facility and remove all waste until a RCRA part B permit was issued.

[c]Violations were found in several areas including groundwater monitoring, the condition of tanks, and compliance with former enforcement actions.

Source: EPA and state environmental compliance and enforcement officials.

Comparison of Health and Safety Violations Found by OSHA and States, 1990-93

Category of violations	Violations detected during task force's inspections	Violations detected after task force's inspections			Total violations detected after task force's inspections
	1990	1991	1992	1993	1991-93
Health and safety training	111	1	1	1	3
Contingency plans	22	0	1	0	1
Workplace surveillance and monitoring	19	1	1	3	5
Potential chemical exposure to workers during incinerator operations and waste handling operations	20	2	0	6	8
General health and safety	148	5	0	5	10
Total violations	**320**	**9**	**3**	**15**	**27**
Total inspections	59[a]	4	1	3	8

Legend

OSHA = Occupational Safety and Health Administration

Note: In 1990, the joint task force detected OSHA violations at 26 of the 29 incineration facilities inspected. Since 1990, 8 of the 29 incinerator units have ceased operating. Since 1990, OSHA conducted 8 inspections at 5 facilities in response to complaints or referrals at the remaining 21 incineration facilities.

[a]OSHA conducted both health and safety inspections during the joint task force's inspections. These are counted as separate inspections.

Source: OSHA and state health and safety inspection officials.

Comments From the Environmental Protection Agency

Note: GAO comments supplementing those in the report text appear at the end of this appendix.

UNITED STATES ENVIRONMENTAL PROTECTION AGENCY
WASHINGTON, D.C. 20460

~~ 2 3 ~~

OFFICE OF
ADMINISTRATION
AND RESOURCES
MANAGEMENT

Mr. Peter F. Guerrero
Director
Environmental Protection Issues
Resources, Community and Economic Development Division
U.S. General Accounting Office
Washington, D.C. 20548

Dear Mr. Guerrero:

I am responding to your October 12 letter requesting the Environmental Protection Agency (EPA) review and comment on a General Accounting Office (GAO) draft report. The draft report is entitled <u>Hazardous Waste Incinerators: EPA and OSHA Action to Better Protect Health and Safety Not Complete</u> (GAO/RCED-95-17). In addition to the general comments below, I have enclosed more specific comments referenced to the draft report.

See comment 1.

Regarding the report's overall conclusions, I recommend that the report discuss additional followup activities initiated by the Office of Solid Waste (OSW). OSW has incorporated improved approaches on emergency safety vents (ESVs) and automatic waste feed cutoffs (AWFCOs) in key program elements. In addition, training for and meetings with combustion permit writers have raised the consciousness of the permit writers.

See comment 2.

It appears that the report misinterprets one of OSW's followup actions -- that OSW would reopen <u>all</u> existing incinerator permits to address AWFCOs and ESVs. Actually, the Task Force recommendation was to reopen permits where the number of AWFCOs and ESV openings was significant.

See comment 3.

The Agency believes that the report should address and clarify EPA's concern and policy on AWFCOs. Our major concern is not with any AWFCO, but with facilities that may have frequent AWFCOs. This is especially true where facilities exceed the permit operating limit after the cutoff, while waste remains in the unit. We do not want to "shield" facilities from violation in such situations because the AWFCO has been activated. Our approach is to write permit requirements so that AWFCO activation does not shield the facility from violation when permit conditions exceedances occur with waste in the unit.

Recycled/Recyclable
Printed with Soy/Canola Ink on paper that
contains at least 50% recycled fiber

2

See comment 4.

Reference to p. 8
now refers to p. 6.

See comment 5.

There is a common misconception that our approach is simply to set a numerical limit on any type of cutoff; we recommend changing the report wording in several places to refer to "controls" on AWFCOs, rather than "limits", to try to clarify this point. This issue is further discussed in the enclosure (see reference to page 8).

The Agency agrees with the recommendation to finalize the guidance on addressing emergency safety vents and automatic waste feed cutoffs. EPA has included this activity in our program plans for Fiscal Year 1995.

Thank you for the opportunity to review and comment on this draft report. I look forward to receiving the final report.

Sincerely,

Jonathan Z. Cannon
Assistant Administrator and
    Chief Financial Officer

Enclosure

Specific Comments
on GAO's Draft Report,
Hazardous Waste Incinerators:
EPA and OSHA Actions to Better Protect
Health and Safety Not Complete (GAO/RCED-95-17)

Now on p. 1.

See comment 6.

Page 2, paragraph 1
Rather than stating that EPA has not fully implemented
recommendations to conduct research, it would be more accurate to
state that, while EPA implemented the recommendation to conduct
research, the initial tests were not sufficient and resources
have not permitted followup testing.

Now on p. 3.

See comment 7.

Page 5, line 2
Delete "1980" and substitute "standards bringing them under RCRA
regulation". (Incinerators gained interim status after 1980 when
new wastes [radioactive mixed waste and wastes exhibiting
toxicity characteristics] became RCRA-regulated. Incinerators
that achieved interim status after the 1984 Hazardous and Solid
Waste Amendments are not subject to the 1989 permitting
deadline.)

Now on p. 5.

See comment 8.

Page 5, last paragraph
In this paragraph, insert the following information: "EPA has
invested considerable resources to establish positions for
specialized hazardous waste combustion inspectors in each Region;
conducted monthly conference calls and annual face-to-face
meetings with inspectors to address issues arising at hazardous
waste incinerators and other combustion facilities; developed
course curriculum for the inspectors; and developed and presented
a new module in the RCRA Inspector Institute on the Task Force
findings to make inspectors more aware of health and safety
concerns."

Now on p. 5.

See comment 9.

Page 6, paragraph 3
Delete "permitting and" in the first sentence. Although there
are combustion permitting experts in the Regions and there are
training sessions and meetings for combustion permitting experts,
these activities originated prior to the EPA/OSHA Task Force.

Now on p. 5.
See comment 10.

Page 7, second paragraph
Add "training courses" after "in EPA's inspection training
manual."

Now on p. 5.
See comment 11.

Page 7, last paragraph
In the first sentence, add "some of the EPA regions...."

2

Now on p. 6.
See comment 12.

Now on p. 6.

See comment 13.

__Page 8, fourth line from the top__
This sentence should read,"...in the training manual and training
courses, EPA believed..."

__Page 8, fifth line from the top__
Please delete this sentence and replace it with the following:
"An EPA Technical Assistance Branch Chief said that it would be
difficult to duplicate the information obtained from the employee
interviews conducted during the Task Force inspection since they
included OSHA and EPA interviews, and were very focused.
However, according to one Regional inspector, while time is a
factor during the inspections, employee interviews could be
routinely included in all inspections or on a case-by-case
basis."

Now on p. 6.

See comment 14.

__Page 8, last sentence on page__
EPA is unaware of any technical basis for the statement that
automatic waste feed cutoffs may lead to vent stack releases.
Recommend deleting this language. Some of the same upset
conditions (e.g., overpressure) that cause an AWFCO may also
cause an emergency vent stack opening, but the act of shutting
off the waste feed itself would not cause a vent stack opening.
Regarding the second part of the sentence, since AWFCOs may be a
sign of unsteady operation, it is conceivable that frequent
AWFCOs may cause the residues to be treated less efficiently.
However, this is not the primary concern with AWFCOs. Therefore,
the Agency recommends that this language be dropped or de-
emphasized.

Recommend inserting the following description of AWFCOs.
Activation is an automatic waste feed cutoff is not in itself a
problem, but frequent cutoffs may be indicative of other
problems. If a permit is written saying an incinerator may only
__feed__ hazardous waste when complying with the operating
conditions, cutting off the waste feed may be construed to
"shield" the facility from being considered in violation, even
though the unit (especially if feeding solids) may still contain
waste after the feed is cut off and the operating parameter may
exceed its permit limit. There would be concern about an
incinerator that has cutoffs frequently that this shielding
effect could allow a significant amount of operational time
outside of the permit operational limits. Further, frequent
AWFCOs are a sign of non-steady-state operation.

See comment 15.

__Page 9, paragraph 1__
The report should clarify that the followup item from the
EPA/OSHA Task Force report was not to revise all existing
incinerator permits. It was to work with states to re-open
permits of facilities with a __significant__ number of bypasses and
AWFCOs.

Now on p. 7.

See comment 16.

3

Now on p. 7.

See comment 17.

Page 9, paragraph 2
In the first sentence, replace "include limit on" with "place proper controls on", so as not to imply that EPA's primary emphasis is to set a numerical limit on AWFCOs or vent stack openings. EPA's primary approach to addressing AWFCOs and vent stack openings is to write permit operating conditions such that the facility must comply as long as there is waste in the unit. This eliminates any violation "shielding" effect. EPA generally feels that numerical limits on cutoffs may only be necessary if the above approach is not sufficient to deter exceedances, or if there is a sufficiently high number of AWFCOs not associated with exceedances to raise concern that the unit is not being operated according to good combustion practice, which includes steady-state operation.

See comment 18.

Regarding the discussion of "other priorities" in the second sentence, the Boiler and Industrial Furnaces (BIF) rule was finalized in 1991. To be more exact, the other priorities included working with the Regions and States on implementing the newly-issued BIF rule, as well as working on site-specific incinerator issues and court cases.

Now on p. 7.

See comment 19.

Page 10, paragraph 1
The correct title in the second sentence is Alternative Technology <u>Section</u> Chief.

Now on p. 7.

See comment 20.

Page 10, second paragraph
Activation of the AWFCO is not in itself a violation. However, it may be <u>associated with</u> a violation if an operating parameter exceedance occurs after a cutoff and waste still remains in the unit. To clarify this, EPA recommends replacing the second half of the first sentence with: "clarify that an exceedance of permit operating parameters, or bypassing the air pollution control device, is a permit violation regardless of whether an automatic waste feed cutoff occurs."

See comment 21.

In addition, EPA recommends revising the end of the third sentence to state "...in issuing permits for existing combustion facilities not yet under final permit controls." The current wording could be construed to mean that the permit prioritization is confined to interim status incinerators. However, interim status BIFs are also a high priority.

Now on p. 8.

See comment 22.

Page 10, third paragraph, last sentence and page 11, first 2 sentences
Just as EPA's Office of Enforcement was "not primarily responsible for conducting inspections or taking enforcement actions at hazardous waste facilities", the new consolidated

4

Office of Enforcement and Compliance Assurance does not undertake these activities. RCRA inspection and enforcement responsibilities have been and continue to be conducted primarily at Regional and State levels. Therefore, Regional and State compliance and enforcement officials are the ones who would carry out the purpose of the September 23, 1994 memorandum referred to earlier. EPA Headquarters can only direct the Regions and suggest that the States do so.

Now on p. 10.
See comment 23.

Page 12, paragraph 1
Clarify the second sentence by inserting "from the Task Force inspections" after..."in scope".

Now on p. 11.
See comment 24.

Page 14, paragraph 3
Insert "Partially" at the beginning of the first sentence.

Now on p. 11.

See comment 25.

Page 15, first partial paragraph, last two sentences
This sentence should read: "EPA also targeted combustion facilities, including ten incinerators and other hazardous waste combustion facilities for two separate enforcement initiatives in September 1993 and February 1994. These initiatives focused primarily on hazardous waste combustion operations and resulted in EPA and States assessing fines of over $9 million."

Now on p. 12.

See comment 26.

Page 16, paragraph 1
In first sentence, delete "Although" and insert "however," after "recommendations".

Now on p. 12.

See comment 27.

page 16, CONCLUSIONS section
To portray the situation more accurately, please revise the discussion starting on the fourth line to read: "In particular, some of the EPA Regions and States have not adopted the use of the revised checklist and employee interview guide." Also, fourth line up from the bottom on page 16 should read, "However, because inspection coverage has not been changed by some Regions to assess..." To address this problem, Steven Herman, the Assistant Administrator for the Office of Enforcement and Compliance Assurance (OECA) issued a September 24, 1994, memorandum to the Regional Administrators requiring the use of such protocol by the Regions and the States in all Compliance and Evaluation Inspections. In addition, Steven Herman requested that all Regions refer violations of these requirements to OSHA as these violations are indicators of likely OSHA violations.

5

Now on p. 12:

Page 17, paragraph 1
As stated above, the Task Force recommendation was not to revise
all permits, but to revise permits where ESV openings and AWFCOs
were significant.

See comment 28.

In the last sentence, replace "limits" with "controls".

Now on p. 12.
See comment 29.

Page 18, paragraph 2
Replace "limit" with "control".

The following are GAO's comments on the Environmental Protection Agency's (EPA) letter dated November 23, 1994.

GAO Comments

1.   We appreciate EPA's efforts to follow up on the task force report's recommendations and believe that the report accurately reflects actions taken by the agency, such as revising permit writers' training to include improved approaches to control the use of emergency safety vents and automatic waste feed cutoffs, thus increasing permit writers' consciousness of this issue.

2.   We have revised the report to clarify that the report did not call for revising all existing incinerator permits but, rather, only those permits where revisions were viewed as necessary because of the high number of safety vents and automatic waste feed cutoffs.

3.   We revised the report to reflect how EPA is addressing the use of automatic waste feed cutoffs in permits, namely, that EPA is placing controls over the use of waste feed cutoffs.

4.   We revised the report to reflect this information.

5.   We revised the report to include this information.

6.   We continue to believe that EPA did not fully implement the recommended research because the recommendation was intended to result in a determination of why waste feed cutoffs and stack vents were used and their impact. We agree that EPA conducted limited tests, but we believe that these initial tests were not sufficient and that limited resources have not allowed the agency to conduct follow-up research to determine the cause and impact of using waste feed cutoffs and stack vents.

7.   We revised the report to include this information.

8.   The report recognizes EPA's efforts to designate and train combustion experts in each region under the caption entitled EPA's Education of Compliance Officials.

9.   We revised the report to limit our discussion to EPA's actions taken after the task force's inspections.

10. We revised the report to include this information.

11. We revised the report to include this information.

12. We revised the report to include this information.

13. We revised the report to include this information.

14. We revised the report to reflect EPA's concerns regarding operating conditions for using automatic waste feed cutoffs and stack vents.

15. We revised the report to clarify this information.

16. The report recognizes that the task force's recommendation was that EPA reopen permits, as necessary, to address the use of automatic waste feed cutoffs and stack vents.

17. We have revised the report to show that EPA's approach is not to impose numerical limits on using waste feed cutoffs or vent stacks but to write permit operating conditions so that the facility must comply with operating conditions as long as waste is present in the unit.

18. We revised the report to reflect EPA's priorities in fiscal year 1992.

19. We revised the report to include this information.

20. We revised the report to clarify that the use of automatic waste feed cutoffs is not in itself a violation.

21. We revised the report to include this information.

22. We have revised the report to reflect the activities of both EPA's Office of Enforcement and OSHA under the memorandum. We continue to believe that the memorandum was not as successful as intended on the basis of information stated in our report.

23. We revised the report to include this information.

24. We revised the report to include this information.

25. We revised the report to include this information.

26.   We revised the report to include this information.

27.   We revised the report to include this information.

28.   We revised the report to include this information.

29.   We revised the report to include this information.

Comments From the Occupational Health and Safety Administration

Note: GAO comments supplementing those in the report text appear at the end of this appendix.

U.S. Department of Labor

Assistant Secretary for
Occupational Safety and Health
Washington, D.C. 20210

NOV 8 1994

Mr. Peter F. Guerrero
Director, Environmental Protection Issues
U.S. General Accounting Office
Washington D.C.   20548

Dear Mr. Guerrero:

Thank you for your letter of October 12 to Secretary of Labor
Robert Reich submitting for our comment your proposed report on
Hazardous Waste Incinerators. The Occupational Safety and Health
Administration (OSHA) appreciates the opportunity to present
comments on this report.

The General Accounting Office (GAO) reviewed the Agency's
participation on a joint OSHA/EPA task force that evaluated
employer compliance with on-site health and safety requirements
at select hazardous waste incinerators. While OSHA, during its
investigation, did not observe evidence of worker overexposure to
chemicals that could cause serious harm, the Agency did notice
widespread deficiencies in the area of worker training.

Thus, the task force report made four recommendations to OSHA.
GAO found that OSHA implemented two of the four recommendations.
These recommendations involved the Agency providing follow up on
violations found during the task force inspections and outreach
to the industry on the Agency's technical services.

See comment 1.

OSHA believes that it responded to the remaining recommendations.
The task force recommended that OSHA improve its inspection
coverage by including hazardous waste incinerators on its lists
of targeted inspections. OSHA at this time targets its limited
enforcement resources on those employers with a past history of
serious OSHA citations. Though the refuse systems industry,
which includes commercial hazardous waste incinerators, does not
currently meet this definition, OSHA does inspect these sites in
response to complaints, fatalities/catastrophes and referrals.

See comment 2.

Also, the task force recommended that OSHA improve the inspection
expertise of its compliance officers in the area of hazardous
waste incineration. OSHA conducts training at its Training
Institute in a course developed to increase inspectors' knowledge
of hazardous waste site operations entitled, "Hazardous Waste
Site Inspection and Emergency Response." To date, 245 Federal
and State compliance officers have received training in this
course.

See comment 3.

See comment 4.

Page 2

Additionally, OSHA compliance officers will receive enhanced knowledge of hazardous waste incinerators and improved inspection expertise through the implementation of an OSHA/EPA Memorandum of Understanding designed to provide a coordinated enforcement effort among other things. In particular, through joint inspections, agency-to-agency referrals, cross-training, and data exchange, both agencies will strengthen their combined efforts to achieve protection of workers, the public, and the environment in hazardous waste incineration and other areas.

Finally, OSHA will soon issue its final rule for Accreditation of Training Programs for Hazardous Waste Operations. When the rule is promulgated, it will require all facilities to obtain accredited training for all new training. Consequently, facilities must either seek out accredited training programs, or submit their own for accreditation. If a facility fails to comply with this rule, or any other OSHA rule, they would be out of compliance and thus subject to OSHA fines and penalties.

OSHA believes that with the implementation of this proposed rule, and its outreach efforts, the quality of employers' safety and health training programs will be greatly enhanced. Such efforts will significantly improve safety and health for workers at waste incinerator sites.

Thank you for your continued efforts to improve safety and health in the workplace. We appreciate the opportunity to work with you in this very important area.

Sincerely,

Joseph A. Dear
Assistant Secretary

The following are GAO's comments on the Department of Labor's letter dated November 8, 1994.

GAO Comments

1. We continue to believe that the Occupational Safety and Health Administration (OSHA) has not implemented the task force's recommendation to improve its coverage of inspections by including hazardous waste incinerators on OSHA's lists of programmed inspections. The task force's recommendation was intended to make sure that hazardous waste incineration facilities were targeted for programmed inspections. However, because of the manner in which OSHA targets high-risk industries for programmed inspections, no incinerators are inspected unless OSHA responds to a complaint, a referral, or an accident. We did not assess or evaluate what impact OSHA's policy for targeting and inspecting high-risk industries has on workers' health and safety and, as such, do not have a position on this policy. Nevertheless, the fact remains that OSHA's choice of actions did not result in the implementation of the task force's recommendation. The only inspections that were performed were in reaction to complaints or referrals. Programmed inspections are broad in scope and are separate from and above OSHA's inspections in response to complaints, referrals, and fatalities/catastrophes, which are more narrow in scope.

2. We continue to believe that OSHA has not implemented the task force's recommendation that OSHA improve its inspection expertise. We have revised the report to point out that we recognize that OSHA does have a training program for its enforcement officials that includes hazardous waste, and while improvements have been made to this training program, none of these improvements were made as a result of the task force's recommendation. Our discussions with officials in OSHA's Training Institute and OSHA's Directorate of Policy and Office of Field Programs reveal that improvements in the training program were not a result of the task force's recommendation.

3. While the 1990 memorandum of understanding between OSHA and the EPA's Office of Enforcement may have the potential for enhancing OSHA's inspection expertise, this memorandum did not result in any such improvement because no joint OSHA-EPA inspections were conducted at incinerators following the task force's inspections. As discussed in the report, EPA's Office of Enforcement did not have oversight responsibilities for regional or state compliance activities at hazardous waste incineration facilities. Also, this office did not provide information to EPA's compliance

staff who were responsible for directing EPA's regional and state compliance activities. Because EPA did not direct EPA regions, the regions did not suggest that states coordinate with OSHA when inspecting combustion facilities, and because no joint inspections occurred after 1990 the memorandum was not fully carried out. Thus, improvements in OSHA's inspection expertise have yet to be demonstrated as a result of the task force's recommendation or this memorandum.

4. We continue to believe that OSHA has no means to ensure that all hazardous waste facilities will have accredited worker training programs. It is the intent of OSHA's new training program standard that all employees working on-site and exposed to hazardous substances will receive OSHA's accredited training. However, as we pointed out, OSHA has no means of ensuring compliance, since (1) OSHA and the states have conducted few inspections at hazardous waste incineration facilities, (2) OSHA considers these facilities a low risk in relation to other industries, and (3) OSHA and the states would inspect these facilities only if they are randomly selected or in response to complaints, referrals, or accidents. Our recommendation that OSHA work with EPA to develop a means of ensuring that all hazardous waste facility employers submit their training programs and receive accreditation could provide OSHA with a more comprehensive means of determining compliance with OSHA's new accreditation requirement.

Scope and Methodology

To review the status of implementing the task force report's recommendations, we obtained documentation on EPA's follow-up actions, education provided to industry, education provided to compliance officials, inspection coverage, research about certain operating equipment, and review of permits from the Resource Conservation and Recovery Act (RCRA) Enforcement and Permits and State Programs Divisions, Office of Research and Development, EPA, and from industry combustion experts. We also obtained documentation on OSHA's follow-up actions, education provided to industry, education provided to compliance officials, inspection coverage, inspection priorities, and field office guidance from staff in OSHA's Directorate of Policy, Office of Statistics and Office of Field Programs.

To determine the results of subsequent inspections and enforcement actions at the 29 facilities we reviewed, we interviewed and obtained documentation on the inspections conducted, violations detected, enforcement actions, and penalties assessed and collected during January 1, 1991, through December 31, 1993, from headquarters' officials in EPA's RCRA Enforcement Division and OSHA's Office of Policy and from cognizant regional and area office officials. We also interviewed and obtained data from state environmental officials in Alabama, Arkansas, Connecticut, Idaho, Illinois, Kentucky, Louisiana, Michigan, Montana, New Jersey, New York, Ohio, South Carolina, and Texas and from state OSHA officials in Kentucky, Michigan, and South Carolina.

To determine other actions taken by EPA and OSHA to improve workers' and the public's health and safety at hazardous waste incineration facilities, we interviewed and obtained documentation on EPA's and the states' enforcement actions and draft waste minimization and combustion strategy, and OSHA's proposed policies and procedures for Hazardous Waste Training Accreditation from (1) EPA's Office of Permits and State Programs and RCRA Enforcement Divisions and (2) OSHA's Directorate of Policy, Office of Health and Safety Standards Program, Office of Field Programs, and Office of Statistics. We conducted our review from September 1993 through December 1994 in accordance with generally accepted government auditing standards.

Major Contributors to This Report

Environmental Protection Issues Area

David W. Bennett, Evaluator
Richard P. Johnson, Attorney
Gerald E. Killian, Assistant Director
Marcia B. McWreath, Evaluator-in-Charge
Rita F. Oliver, Evaluator
James L. Rose, Evaluator
Bernice Steinhardt, Associate Director